FREE STUFF

HOW OTHERS GET FREE MONEY, BOOZE, GASOLINE, AND EVERYTHING!

JOHN GREEN

PALADIN PRESS
BOULDER, COLORADO

Free Stuff:
How Others Get Free Money, Booze, Gasoline, and Everything!
by John Green

CONTENTS

INTRODUCTION

ere are more than fifty ways that have been used by people to get free money, travel, food, clothes, electrical goods, and more. These are techniques that have been used out of necessity, or out of a desire to stack up a few points against companies and organizations that traditionally rob people blind anyway, or simply because someone got plain bored one day and decided to see if things really could still be had for free in today's high-tech world of computer credit checks and surveillance cameras.

The answer, by the way, is yes, they can.

Many of the techniques are perfectly legal, some are not, and several are "borderline." Because of this, no one is suggesting that you actually do these things, and the book should be looked upon simply as entertainment.

Of course, if circumstances should ever conspire to create the necessity, if your stack of points is running low, or if you are feeling particularly bored, well . . .

FREE ADMISSION TO RALLIES, FAIRS, AND SHOWS

Free admission to any number of rallies and "whateverfests" is available provided that some form of ticket or sticker is given by the organizers at the door to prove that a visitor has paid the admittance fee. All you need to do is approach people leaving the site and ask if they are finished with their ticket/sticker/half ticket. The overwhelming majority of people will hand it over with a smile. The parking lot will, in any case, be littered with used tickets so if you would rather not ask, then simply do your bit for litter control and pick up one or two.

In areas where people actually use litter bins, lift a couple of tickets from these (under cover of throwing something away, of course!). When entering the show, simply flash the ticket, half ticket, or sticker and, should anyone actually bother to ask, explain that you went out to put something in your car or whatever.

An alternative that is applicable for some situations is to have a few friends pool their money to buy one or two tickets and then, once they are inside, place the ticket in a cigarette packet or empty soft drink can that is then thrown over a perimeter fence or such to the others waiting outside. The process can be repeated as often as required.

For shows where the hands of people leaving temporarily are stamped with an ink design, a similar technique can be used inasmuch as at least one ticket is purchased. The purchaser then exits temporarily, having had his or her hand stamped. Out of sight of the gate staff, the stamped hand is sprayed lightly with WD-40 and then pressed against a sheet of white paper, which has been folded over a bundled-up handkerchief. This paper/handkerchief pad is now pressed onto the hand of another person.

Note that if the ink is so weak that it renders this technique unusable, then simply drawing a rough approximation of the design onto a hand with a felt-tipped pen and smudging it usually will be enough to gain admittance. If it is known that a simple date stamp will be used, it is possible to obtain a duplicate one from most any custom stamp shop. A simple child's printing set can also be purchased and used, as the majority of likely checkout (or check-in) designs can be replicated with one.

FREE ADVERTISING

Free advertising is available in the numerous free papers found at large supermarkets, service stations, and so on. Invariably, a condition of the ad being free is that it must be a private rather than trade or business ad. Such ads are, of course, used by many small (and even some quite large) businesses, since checks are rarely, if ever, made. So if you don't have anything to sell, place a free ad offering to take things away for free.

This isn't as ridiculous as it might sound. A substantial number of companies exist that do nothing but charge people to remove unwanted items, which are then sold at a profit. If your ad pulls a pile of requests to move anything that is unpleasant or unlikely to prove profitable, simply apologize and explain that your vehicle is booked solid for the next six months. Once you have obtained a few free items, place another free ad elsewhere offering them for sale.

The high costs of advertising in many glossy magazines and newspapers can be avoided completely by having some single-sheet flyers printed up and paying delivery boys a few dollars to let you insert one in each copy of whatever they are delivering. Flyers can also be placed in library books for subsequent discovery by readers.

Free ads can also be had by writing letters under an assumed name to magazines that are targeted at users of your product or service, explaining how the service/product provided by your company/yourself was particularly good. With so many fly-by-night companies around, you felt you simply must share this good news with fellow readers.

FREE AFTER-SHAVE AND PERFUME

Free after-shave and perfume are available on a daily basis from most large department stores in the form of a dab or spray or two from the various sampler bottles left open to attract would-be purchasers. Pass through on your way to work or home and you can smell like a million dollars for free.

The larger after-shave and perfume suppliers will also have allocated to most stores any number of small sample bottles. These are usually given away with purchases of a full-size bottle of some related product, but if you dress as if you can afford it, and if you ask nicely, you will be given a few samples to take away and evaluate.

FREE AIR TRAVEL

The first technique here is usable only if you are actually intending to go somewhere anyway and would quite like to get more free travel and/or some cash as a bonus. There is no guarantee that it will work all the time and, indeed, the very nature of the technique means that it can't possibly work for everybody all the time. I can honestly say, however, that it has worked for someone I know personally a few times, and very recently.

Book your flight as usual but turn up at the check-in desk at the very last minute, i.e., the latest publicized check-in time. If the flight is a popular one, the odds are in your favor that you will be bumped off—that is, there will be no room for you on the flight because the seat has been given to someone else.

It is common airline practice to sell more seats than they actually have available on a given flight because they know from long experience that a percentage of passengers will not turn up on the day of the flight. When everybody does turn up, they have no option but to offer the "unfortunate" traveler a seat on a later flight. As long as the traveler was not to blame, this invariably will be accompanied by a cash refund and/or a free ticket. If you are rarely in a hurry to get where you are going, then turning up at the last minute rather than being first in line can pay dividends. It's possible to confirm beforehand whether a specific flight is fully booked by inquiring by phone at your local discount air fare shop at regular intervals after you have purchased your own ticket. Airlines frequently offer special deals which enable people to obtain flights for free (i.e., buy one, get one free) but advertise them only within the traveling community. Thus, if you aren't using the airline you won't (normally) hear about the special deals. If travel is on the horizon, then it is worthwhile to phone a few carriers and ask if they have any special offers available.

Of course, you can travel practically for free simply by booking through one of the discount air fare shops rather than a regular travel agency. Forget charter flights, just ask for the cheapest scheduled flight available to wherever on such and such a date. If you are used to booking through the big-name agencies, you will be amazed at the savings. There are certain limitations concerning the length of stay and the period the flight must be booked in advance, but these rarely are a problem. The savings possible on long-haul flights really do mean that if a couple of you are traveling together one is practically travelling for free.

The ticket system for short-hop national flights (and long-haul international flights that stop off at a couple of points en route) has also been manipulated by people so that at least part of the journey is obtained for free. Note now that in the case of long-haul flights with short stops, the passenger using the technique would have no check-in luggage, only carryons.

For short-hop flights, the technique is to purchase two tickets from different sources. Although both tickets are for the same flight, one is for one of the shorter legs and the other is for the final destination. This latter ticket is purchased in the traveler's real name, the former under a fictitious name.

At the check-in desk, the first ticket is presented. It will be processed as usual and returned by way of a receipt in an airline envelope along with a boarding pass. Once aboard, the receipt is removed from the envelope and destroyed. The ticket with the real name is carefully torn out so that only the receipt page remains. This receipt for the final destination is placed in the issued envelope and the ticket is pocketed.

When the appropriate short-hop leg is completed, the traveler simply remains seated. Flight attendants generally assume that if a passenger isn't disembarking he is ticketed for the next leg. If questions are asked, then a genuine receipt for the final destination can, of course, be produced.

The second ticket and receipt would ultimately be reunited and offered for a refund or exchange. Questions as to why the pages had become detached would be fended off with any number of plausible excuses (the actions of an inquisitive child, the traveller himself through ignorance of how the tickets should be offered at check-in, and so on).

For long-haul international flights with intermediate stops (as opposed to overnight stopovers), a similar technique has been used. Here, however, only one ticket is purchased, which is to the first or second of the intermediate stops. No ticket manipulation is employed, and the idea is simply to stay on board the flight until the final destination is reached. If passengers are required to disembark at these intermediate stops so that the aircraft may be cleaned and refueled, a new boarding/transit passenger pass will be offered as the aircraft is exited. At many such stops on international flights, the cabin crew will change, making the likelihood of anyone asking awkward questions doubly unlikely. This technique is only likely to fail if the flight is booked to capacity and everyone actually turns up.

▼

FREE ANTIQUE EVALUATIONS AND INSURANCE APPRAISALS

The vast majority of "name" auction houses and quite a few of the smaller ones offer a free evaluation service on items taken to their premises, usually between set hours on a specific day of the week. This is a good way to get an idea of the value of certain antique and collectible pieces (for resale or insurance purposes), especially the ones you obtained free by reading the next section.

▼

FREE ANTIQUES

Antiques frequently turn up in the items donated to charity shops. These are the shops that sell bric-a-brac and other merchandise cheaply to raise money for their specific organization.

In many of these shops the staff are unpaid volunteers. They sort donated articles, price them, and put them on display. By volunteering to help for a day or half a day a week, or even on an as-needed basis, you will get the pick of any potentially profitable items.

The few dollars you will donate to the charity in return for the things you take ('cause you're honest) will be a small investment compared to the price the majority of antiques/collectibles will fetch when sold on the collector's market. If you have no idea what is collectible these days, borrow a few books on the subject from the library and I guarantee you will be amazed. One man's junk really is another man's treasure.

FREE BOOKS

Most publishers will be only too pleased to place you on their mailing list for promotional copies of new releases. Simply prepare a letterhead which identifies you as a book club or magazine editor. If you have access to a simple home computer/desktop publishing package, you can guarantee the continued supply of new releases by typing up a "review" and sending a copy of it, along with a thank-you note, to the publishers in question.

The majority of libraries will give you free books at least once a year when they have their annual clear-out. They may offer them cheaply in some sort of sale first, but if any remain unsold or in cases where sales are likely to prove unprofitable anyway, they will throw them out or give them to whomever can provide the best story, e.g., they are for a charity, are to be sent overseas to poor kids, etc.

Mail-order book clubs frequently advertise special membership offers which entitle you to at least one free book regardless of whether you ultimately join or not. Watch for such ads and send in coupons for only those that do not commit you to a membership immediately. Usually the gist of the offer will be that in return for a little under three dollars you will receive four books of your choice from the advertised list. If you eventually decide that you don't want to keep them and don't want to join, you can return three of them at the club's expense and keep the fourth yourself.

All you do is read three of them, return them as per the offer, and put the fourth on your bookshelf. If, having explained that you don't want to be a member after all, you still receive books on a "review" basis, don't pay for them and don't send them back. There is no legal obligation for you to pay for anything you didn't order and no reason you should put yourself out to return them unless you are suitably compensated for your time and effort.

FREE BOOZE

Free bottled beer has been obtained by determined folk in the following manner. A six-pack of bottled beer (or three) is purchased as usual from wherever. The beer is selected for its bottle, which is of the crimped-cap type without fancy sealing foil.

The beer is taken home, removed from the cardboard carrier, and opened—not, however, with a bottle opener, but by levering up just enough of the cap edge to facilitate its contents' removal. The beer is consumed. Water is now poured into the bottle and the cap replaced. The levered-up edges are crimped back down with a pair of nutcrackers or large pliers. The bottles are replaced in the carrier and then returned to the store with an apology and an extremely polite request to change them for a different brand. Don't forget the receipt. Explain that you were told to buy the beer for a party but selected the wrong brand.

It is worth mentioning that suppliers of home-brew beer and wine equipment carry proper cap-crimping tools and a variety of different colored caps!

In most casinos in Las Vegas and elsewhere, as long as you are gambling you will be served as many free drinks as you can stomach, the theory being that the drunker you get, the dumber you'll be and the more of your hard-earned cash will end up in the casino's coffers. The trick is to park yourself at a low-stakes blackjack table and ride out your $10 or $20 worth of $2 chips as long as possible, ordering a drink every time the cocktail waitress makes her rounds. Be sure to tip her now and again to ensure her continuous attention. To make your pile last as long as possible, befriend others at the table who seem to know what they're doing (i.e., those with the biggest pile of chips) and either mimic their playing style or solicit their advice outright. If all goes well, you should be able to guzzle $50 to $100 worth of free booze, enjoy a little entertainment while you drink, and maybe even win a few bucks!

FREE BUFFET MEALS

These are regularly held by television companies for members of the press with a view to promoting some new series or season of programs. Photos and publicity material will be available, as will free food and wine. Drop a couple of letters to some stations and explain that you are the television reviewer for a new local newspaper or magazine and ask how one goes about getting on the promotion list.

Buffet lunches and dinners also are often held in hotels by companies and organizations. Although you probably will need a ticket to get in if you arrive close to the proper start time, if you show up when things are in full swing or when most people have eaten and are now standing around chatting, you usually will be able to walk straight in and help yourself to what is left. The first thing to do on entering the room is to grab a glass. Always act confidently and, if questioned (very unlikely anyway), explain that you are a friend of "John's."

If you live near or are visiting a dock area from which sea cruise ships depart, you might also take advantage of the fact that a running buffet often is available for passengers and their guests. It is unusual for friends of passengers not to be allowed on board to see them off, and as ship security is rarely as tight as airline security, there should be little problem in getting on board.

If questioned, say you are there to see the Smiths off.

Assuming you are smartly dressed and politely spoken, you could even approach a suitable-looking party and explain that you have always wanted to look around a big ship but your funds have never allowed it. Could you possibly come on board with them? You'll carry their bags, if they like, please, huh?

FREE BUS RIDES

This technique might not get you very far, but it is free so what do you expect? It is suitable for use on pay-as-you-enter city buses. All you do is get on the bus at a bad traffic spot, i.e., a point where the driver wants to pull over for as brief a period as possible and then get back out into traffic again. Try to time your entrance to coincide with him just closing the door.

As he pulls away, pretend to be looking for change and then ask if this bus goes to wherever (you know, of course, that it doesn't). "Hell no," will be the reply, and the driver will look around for somewhere safe to drop you off. Engage him in conversation about the idiot that gave you the wrong directions and apologize for the inconvenience. Expect to travel a few hundred yards to a quarter mile or so, depending on the attitude of the driver and the road layout.

On ticketed routes, paying for a ticket to some point on the way to your real destination and then "sleeping through the stop" is another old favorite that still works in most places. If "awoken," simply act surprised and confused. Never apologize. After all, what have you done wrong? You're the guy who's missed his stop, right?

FREE CANNED FOOD

anned food that has a paper label is used here. All you do is purchase a can of your favorite brand and, very carefully, pierce a tiny hole in the side just beneath the label. Leave in a warm place for a few days and then open just enough to reveal the contents, which should be nicely "off" by then.

Return the can (sealed in a plastic bag and packed in a small box) to the manufacturer with a note explaining when and where it was purchased and how you were very surprised and shocked to see that it was contaminated. Explain that you have been buying their products for some time but this has put you off. Note that some manufacturers require you only to return a label along with a specific reason for dissatisfaction in order to secure a replacement. In the vast majority of cases, the replacement (which may be the product itself or a redeemable certificate) will be accompanied by samples of other products.

Canneries will often let you have a box or two of dented cans for free, especially if you explain that you represent some charity that provides free meals for the needy. Visit the plant armed with some suitable I.D. and ask to speak to the manager or foreman. In many cases you will find that an invitation will be made to call at a certain time each week to collect the food. This you would welcome, of course, and thank the manager on behalf of the unfortunate needy folk. If your conscience bothers you, donate half of what you get to a genuine charitable food distribution group and sleep easy.

▼

FREE CAR AND TRUCK RENTAL

Here we are talking about car and truck rental deals in which the mileage is charged at X amount per mile, either from the word go or after an agreed limit.

The technique is to keep an eye on the mileage you are clocking up and, when it reaches a few miles short of the limit, stop and disconnect the speedometer. This will disable the odometer, too. All the miles you now cover before reconnecting the speedo will be free save for the cost of gas. Be sure to reconnect it before returning the vehicle.

Disconnection methods will vary slightly from vehicle to vehicle. If the odometer is driven by a cable, it will be visible from the underside of the vehicle in the form of a flexible drive cable connected to the side of the engine or gearbox. Disassembly requires nothing more than unclipping a plastic retainer and/or undoing a small nut. With the clip/nut free, the cable can be pulled clear and fastened in place with duct tape or cord.

Reassembly is a reversal of the above, with the inner drive part of the cable inserted into the opening and the clip/nut retightened.

More sophisticated vehicles may sport an electronic system. These can be bypassed by removing any applicable fuse or, having cross-referenced the location in the owner's manual (present as a matter of course in most rental vehicles), by simply pulling off a connector or such. Doing this on such electronic systems often will disable some other feature as well, but it will not interfere with the vital accessories such as lights, direction indicators, etc. Remember to replace before returning the vehicle.

This technique can also be used to good effect when you want to use a company vehicle (the mileage of which is closely monitored) for private purposes.

▼

FREE CAR
SPARE PARTS

Rental vehicles are used by some people as a source of spare parts ranging from bulbs to carburetors. A vehicle of a similar make to yours is rented and the switch made before it is returned. Some of the things that can be exchanged without causing undue concern on the part of the rental company include carburetors (any date seals, etc., are switched between the newer carb and the older one), air and fuel filters, brake pads, headlamp and indicator bulbs, and fuses. In fact, any item that might legitimately have become worn, blown, or burnt out during the course of the hire is fair game.

An alternate technique is to purchase a needed replacement part such as a carburetor and then replace its innards with the worn innards from an old unit. The part is returned within the required time limit with an explanation that someone else had gone out and bought a replacement at the same time.

Here again, this technique has been used with any number of items that have removable innards. Of course care is taken to ensure that no signs of tampering remain.

▼

FREE CAR WASH

Several garages offer a free car wash token with gasoline purchases over a given amount. Keep your eyes open for this offer the next time you need to fill up. An alternative is to purchase a token for the car wash from the cashier and then return a few seconds later explaining that it went straight into the machine and nothing happened. Is it a joke? Was it the wrong token? In the vast majority of cases another token will be handed over with a smile.

▼

FREE CHOCOLATES

Choose an expensive box of the type that might be purchased for a present and open as usual. If there is an attached gift card, write it out for some friend or relative. Eat a couple of the chocolates. Good, huh! Now bite off a piece of fingernail or grab a few hairs from your hairbrush. Select a chocolate and bite partway through it. Remove from your mouth and insert the nail or hair pieces. Return the whole package to the manufacturer, attention of the Customer Service Department, detailing when and where you purchased it. Mention how it was a gift and that the recipient was extremely distressed to find the foreign body therein. Add that you have been buying X brand chocolates for years and have always found them to be of excellent quality. You don't want a refund—the money isn't the point—but you felt that you should let them know.

Expect to receive a full or at least partial selection of all chocolates the company in question makes or a gift certificate for the same and a letter of apology. In any event, the replacement value of the chocolates will be more than adequately covered. Reply to the letter expressing gratitude and explaining that your faith in the company is restored.

▼

FREE CIGARETTE LIGHTERS

Free disposable lighters and matches can be secured by dropping a line to promotional gift companies (see ads in "Bargain Buy" type magazines or the Yellow Pages) and explaining that you are interested in having several hundred such items produced as Christmas gifts for employees. As usual, decent letterhead will work wonders. Expect a sample of one of each related product that the company in question offers.

Vary the letter slightly so as to show that you are a printer and send to manufacturers/distributors of products that can be printed on for promotional use. Explain that you are interested in offering this service to your customers and would like to check out the quality of available items.

Free lighters can also be had in the form of discarded disposable types, as many of these can be refilled and the flint replaced. If the base of the discarded lighter has a central hollow in which there's a small black sealing plug, the odds are that it can be refilled. Use the gas canister without any of the nozzles fitted and press hard. Some gas will be lost, but enough will force its way past the plug to refill the lighter.

To see if the flint is replaceable, grab the flint wheel firmly and pull. If it comes out you should see the flint tensioner screw on the bottom of the flint spring holder. Many disposable lighters are, in fact, thus designed by virtue of their cheapness rather than because they cannot be refilled or have a new flint installed. Check before you throw yours away, or collect a few from friends, refill and reflint them, and sell them.

▼

FREE CIGARETTES

Although extremely unfashionable these days, cigarette smoking is a habit difficult to break. Since it can also be expensive, a supply of free cigarettes might be a good idea. These can be obtained by writing to any large tobacco company, addressing the letter to the attention of the Product Development Department.

The majority of tobacco companies offer willing parties the opportunity to evaluate various new brands or mixes at home. Nowadays, you will probably be required to sign a declaration absolving the company from blame should you contract some smoking-related disease, and you will have to be over eighteen years of age. Expect cigarettes approximately at monthly intervals. Complete and return the accompanying evaluation form and the supplies, although not large, should keep coming.

FREE CINEMA AND THEATER TICKETS

A visit to the cinema or theater manager before or after show hours will frequently turn up trumps if you explain that you are the new reviewer for some magazine or newspaper. Mention the benefits of free publicity for the cinema and imply or state outright (depending on the initial reaction of the manager) that should you find it impossible to review a film or play positively, you will not review it at all. In other words, for nothing more than the cost of a ticket (which doesn't really cost him anything at all) he can depend on good, free publicity.

An alternative approach is to pay a visit to the theater box office and inquire about a free pass for any forthcoming shows. Most theaters usually have a few promotional tickets to play with and will be happy to let you have one or two. Writing to a specific cast member, care of the theater, can also have excellent results, especially if you select someone other than the obvious star. Explain what a fan you are but the cost of the ticket is a bit beyond you at the moment. Always ask for an autograph when you do this.

You can also combine these techniques. Write to the specific cast member explaining that not only are you a big fan but you would also like to arrange an interview before the show for publication in some local magazine. Expect a letter and pass or a note to the effect that your name and a pass will be left at the stage door. If you get this far, use the opportunity to make friends with the doorman, manager, and anyone else likely to be of future use.

Through research and a couple of phone calls (maybe under the pretext of finding out who you should write to about a job, for example), you should be able to find out the name of the general manager or some other senior management member of a theater or cinema chain. Armed with this information, phone the individual cinema or theater and claim to be calling from the head office on behalf of the management member. Explain that he or she has a couple of very important out-of-town visitors who will be passing through that area tonight and would like to visit the cinema/theater. Ask for a couple of "complimentaries" to be left at the box office for them. When you turn up at the theater, walk confidently to the front of any line and say something like, "Guests of Mr./Ms. Whomever."

▼

FREE CLOTHES

Free clothes can be obtained easily from stores that have a refund or replacement policy. This is a nice way of getting the chance to wear expensive designer clothes without having to buy them. Maybe there is some special party or a holiday that warrants some special gear, whatever.

Visit the store and purchase the selected item/s. Remove the tags carefully and keep the receipt. Wear the clothes, taking reasonable care not to ruin them, and, a few days or weeks later, return them with an appropriate explanation, having first replaced the tags.

The explanation might be anything from the wrong size to a duplicated gift. If the time between purchase and return has been quite lengthy, explain that you have been away on business or on vacation. Several larger stores permit returns to any of its branches. Thus you can exchange clothes for free in a completely different state.

Most of the larger clothing stores also have in-house sales for employees only. At such sales it is possible to obtain clothing at a massive discount. If you can find someone who works at such a place, it is possible to arrange a deal whereby they purchase discounted clothes, sell them to you at a nominal profit, and you return them to the store for a refund or replacement, which might then be sold at even more of a profit.

It is also possible to purchase certain types of clothes (brand-name jeans, for example) at discount stores and then return them to a different store for a refund or replacement. The price difference is your free profit. Several stores will exchange goods without a receipt, but if this is not store policy, then opening an account beforehand will help ensure a positive reaction. Receipts could otherwise be obtained from friends who have purchased a similar article of clothing, or by purchasing some lesser item and tearing the receipt so that only the date and store name (or other identifying symbols) are retained and not the item description itself. Many receipts are now stapled to the bag when a purchase is made, so finding an excuse for having a torn receipt is not hard.

Yet another variation is to purchase something having a value the same as that of an item you will be returning. The merchandise to be returned is purchased cheaply elsewhere and then returned with the genuine store receipt for a refund. A quick glance through a clothing retailer trade magazine will turn up ads for specialty tools and plastic clips of the type used to secure tags to clothing. These can prove useful in many of the projects outlined above!

Free clothes can also be had by collecting, as for a rummage sale, in high-class areas. Here you will find any number of expensive items being donated gratis, especially if you mention that the proceeds are to be used for some worthy cause.

Free T-shirts are frequently available from companies promoting films, events, and products at trade shows. Keep an eye out for ads for such shows in the national press and in specialist publications. A list of such publications, as well as book publishers and other useful addresses, can be found in *Literary Market Place* (*LMP*) and other reference books for writers and artists.

By the way, although access to many trade shows (which cover everything from electronics to food) is by invitation only, more often than not all you need to do to get an invitation is fill in a coupon in one of the trade magazines, giving details of your company and position, or contact the organizers directly. Very frequently, the invitation is included in the magazine itself and you simply clip it out and take it along to the show. It always pays to wear a suit to such events and to carry a briefcase.

Wearing a badge bearing your company name and your position will guarantee a plentiful supply of free samples, brochures, and the like. Use the opportunity to spread the name of your company amongst exhibitors and thereby ensure even more invites to trade fairs in the future.

▼

FREE COLLECTIONS

An instant collection of most anything can be obtained simply by writing a few letters or placing a few ads. For collections of ties, badges, baseball caps, T-shirts, buttons, and anything else that is traditionally used for advertising a service, product, or company name, write (don't type) to all the large companies you can find advertising in the Yellow Pages or wherever and explain that you are a child who collects whatever. Have they any examples they could let you have, please? Always write back and thank them.

When placing an ad for free things, always use emotional hooks such as "Wanted for child's collection" or "Disabled collector seeks" or "Wanted by old-age pensioner" or even "Unemployed collector seeks."

▼

FREE COMPACT DISCS

Free CDs can be obtained by answering any of the numerous advertisements for clubs found in magazines and newspapers. Go for the sort of deal that gives you, for example, four CDs for ninety-nine cents when you become a member. Complete the form with your own or, preferably, a mail drop address but do not sign the obligation to buy X number of discs per month at the full price for the specified period.

A few will ignore the application and a few will write and request you sign the form before they send the discs, but some will send the discs anyway along with a request that you sign and return the form as soon as possible. Instead, write and explain that you don't want to be a member after all. As you have not signed the form, there exists no legally binding contract and although you might get hassled by mail to return the discs, the matter will not be taken further. A variation on this sort of offer is to allow you to keep one disc anyway if, when you get the other discs, you don't want them and don't want to be a member. Frequently you will be able to return the unwanted discs at the company's expense.

Another way to manipulate this type of club is to buy the required amount of discounted CDs per year or whatever, and then "return" them to a store selling the same titles at the full price for a refund or credit.

▼

FREE COMPUTER SOFTWARE

A mass of free computer software is available from the numerous computer bulletin boards that can be accessed by anyone with a computer/modem/phone setup. In reality, these free programs often are of the "shareware" type and are obtained on the condition that, if you find the program useful and intend to keep on using it, you are trusted to send a payment to the author. The specific cost and address details accompany all such programs.

Funny thing is, sometimes it can take forever to decide if one wants to keep the program or not, and therefore whether one should send off the payment. I've been using some software for three years now and I'm still not sure if it's useful!

As a means of encouraging payment, several such programs incorporate a time-delay effect that will "short-circuit" the program so that, without inputting some password or without having had the delay removed by the author (upon payment), the actual use of the program is limited. In order to overcome these problems, there are other programs available that enable the user to trace the sequence of events as the shareware program runs. Using this, it is possible to see what line of instruction is responsible for the short-circuit and remove it.

As bulletin board operators (SYSOPS, or System Operators) don't like hundreds of people downloading software without uploading (into the system) software for use by others, they frequently limit the size of programs that can be downloaded without a corresponding upload. This can be circumvented to some extent by signing on as a new user each time you use the bulletin board. Remember to keep a note of the different names and passwords you use!

An alternative (once your download limit is reached) is simply to upload some of the stuff you downloaded originally. This certainly isn't in keeping with the spirit of the system, but it will be sufficiently within the letter of the requirements to cause the bulletin board to note the byte value of your upload and allocate you a proportionately higher download limit.

FREE CONDOMS

ree condoms are available from the local health department and various family planning clinics found in most cities. Check the phone book for the address of one closest to you or, more useful perhaps, one not so close to you. Many areas have laws concerning the supplying of birth control products to persons under eighteen years of age, but since a primary purpose of such clinics is to prevent underage pregnancies anyway, there rarely will be a problem. Expect a lecture on birth control and a fistful of leaflets.

Condoms are also available from mobile distribution centers often found in known red-light areas. Free syringes are also available from this source, but you will have to mix with some pretty weird types to get them. My advice is to put a condom on first before visiting such projects.

▼

FREE ELECTRICITY

Electricity is available for free perfectly legally in the form of homemade generators or batteries. The former may be wind or mechanically powered, while the latter may be readily constructed from any number of scrap bits and pieces. The plans for do-it-yourself generators can be found advertised in numerous electronic hobbyist magazines. Excellent plans for batteries and generators are available from the company Information Unlimited, which advertises regularly in the classified pages of *Soldier of Fortune* magazine and elsewhere.

You might even think about installing a small turbine-type generator in a water pipe. The higher the pressure available in the pipe, the better. Every time the tap is used, the turbine vanes turn and generate a small but usable current. This might be used to keep nicad batteries charged, for example. Rumor also has it that the voltage/current available from the phone line (before you dial any number and incur a charge) is useable for trickle-charging small batteries. I have not confirmed this, but the electronic hobbyists amongst you might want to investigate the idea further.

A perfectly legal but unfortunately very unreliable method of obtaining free electricity has been mentioned by a few people. It seems to work only where there exists a combination of modern electronic equipment and an older type of electricity meter. Other things being equal, modern electronic equipment consumes far less current than was the case a few years ago, and it is possible, given the right combination of equipment and meter, to run a single item without the meter actually registering. It might be worthwhile to experiment by switching off all appliances and then turning them back on one by one to see if this does happen. It most definitely will not work with obvious high-current electrical equipment like heaters, washing machines, etc.

Various "black boxes" and designs for same can be found advertised in electronic hobbyist magazines. These devices will slow, stop, or, if you are particularly unfortunate, reverse the meter.

Meters can also be slowed or stopped if a powerful magnet is positioned in front of the rotating disk glass. This could happen accidentally if a suitable magnet were resting on a wooden stepladder, which itself had been left leaning carelessly against the meter. Make sure you never allow this to happen. If the meter disk were accidentally stopped in this manner, it should be noted that it sometimes might not start again, even when the magnet is removed. Should this occur, the power should be switched off at the fuse box, several high-current electrical appliances switched on, and then the power switch itself thrown on again. This has the effect of "kicking" the disk back to life.

FREE ELECTRONIC SPARE PARTS

This is a technique with various permutations. In its basic form it relates to a scenario in which your early model X computer has a worn-out disk drive but, as you are upgrading anyway, you don't want to spend money on a new drive before selling it. Yes, the warranty has expired. You pop down to the local dealer, purchase the new model X (which has the same disk drive as the previous model), return, disassemble both drives, and replace the worn one in the new machine. Care will be taken, as always, not to damage the machine or make it overly obvious that you have disassembled anything. You now wait a couple of days and then return the new machine, complaining that the disk drive is stuffed.

Most large retailers will give the drive a quick test and then replace the machine. The machine probably will not even be sent away for repair; it will be sold as faulty, since the cost of determining and repairing faults, service charges being what they are, exceeds the unit's profit margin. I know of this sort of technique being used on everything from expensive, single semiconductors to computers and printers. I daren't name the stores it is easiest to play this game with, as they might just change their sales policies! Suffice to say it should work with any large, international supplier/retailer that employs staff who are not part owners in the company.

One variation (applicable to other items as well as electronic systems) is to have friends keep you apprised of any products they are going to purchase of a type that you have already had for some time. They buy it from a store that has a refund or replacement facility and, within a few days, return your item as if it were theirs. Very few companies check serial numbers, and even if they do these can be swapped over easily enough. As long as the item is of the same type and is in good condition physically, there will be no problems.

▼

FREE EXPENSES

Persons whose employment requires them to claim expenses incurred during the course of their work frequently abuse the system by turning in exaggerated or completely faked receipts. The most common technique used with legitimately obtained handwritten receipts is simply to add or otherwise alter a figure to the total shown. Thus, for example, on a receipt for food or gasoline showing a total of thirteen dollars, the figure 3 would be changed to an 8. A 1 might be changed to a 4, 6, 9 or 11, and so on.

Such changes are to be made so as not to stretch the realms of credibility with the accounting staff; thus the figure 14 would not be changed to read 114 even though this could be accomplished simply by adding a 1.

The technique works because, although the figures are handwritten, the receipt will bear a legitimate company stamp and the additions made are within probable limits anyway. Even the most casual of company accountants will raise an eyebrow if the food expenses for one salesman are hundreds of dollars greater than other employees (other things being equal), but not if they vary by only a few dollars. These few dollars add up, of course, and therefore are worth investing a little time in to secure.

Sales reps and others will befriend certain gas station and restaurant employees and thereby obtain blank receipts which subsequently can be filled in to suit. Likewise, receipt books in the name of a fictitious establishment can be printed up professionally or blank receipt books purchased and a suitable company stamp purchased.

Where applicable (as is the case with many types of tax return requirements), receipts pertaining to some personal, nonclaimable items may be submitted as relating to business or other reclaimable expenses. This technique works if the receipt is obtained from a store that sells a variety of merchandise and does not specify the specific products on its receipts. An example would be the purchase of a novel from a bookstore that also sells account books for small businesses. The receipt does not specify the exact nature of the purchase and thus may be submitted as "proof" of a legitimate business purchase, i.e., the account book/s. Similarly, the receipt for the purchase of a set of new tires for a personal vehicle could be submitted as relating to a pickup truck used purely for business.

Friends could also give you receipts that are of no use to them but are valuable to you. This is especially applicable in situations where you are in a position to claim back expenses incurred in the provision of business lunches and such.

Vehicle mileage allowance payments might also be exaggerated simply by advancing the odometer reading via an electric drill attached to the speedometer drive cable. Here the drive cable is detached from the underside of the vehicle, the inner section of the cable tightened into the drill jaws, and power applied. The ready availability of cordless drills makes this technique even easier than it used to be.

Where gasoline receipts cannot be altered and in situations where an employer has an account with a certain garage so that you do not have to pay when filling up, gasoline itself is obtained for free by covertly filling a petrol can or two every time the vehicle tank is topped off. The simple alternative to this is to siphon a gallon or two a day from the vehicle and transfer it to your own vehicle at some later time.

FREE EXTRA
WHATEVERS

These are the things that come as accessories or con-
sumables when you buy certain other things. Clear
as mud, huh! It's difficult to categorize them but an
example would be a boxed staple gun. These typi-
cally are supplied in a box containing the stapler itself and a selection of staples. Usually one of the boxes will be open and on display in the store, but the one you purchase is in an unopened box.

All you do is buy the merchandise as usual, then return a few
hours later with the item and your receipt and explain that when
you opened the box there were no staples in it. Look, you can see
for yourself, the space is empty. The vast majority of stores will
simply assume that the package came from the factory like that
and give you a replacement. Thus you have an extra set of staples
for free. The technique is applicable to any such item that is supplied boxed and not checked before you leave the store.

A reverse variation I have seen used quite often is to buy an
item needed only for one specific job from any store that offers an
X-day guaranteed refund like, for example, a home carpet cleaner. The cleaner is purchased as normal, the carpet cleaned, and the
unit then returned with an explanation that it just wasn't powerful
enough or whatever. A refund is obtained and the cleaning project
has been obtained for a fraction of the cost of renting a machine or
hiring someone else to do the job.

The employees at such stores don't care, and if the store wants to offer that policy, why not take advantage of it?

▼

FREE FAKE I.D.

Free fake I.D. cards and the like can be obtained by writing to printers and producers of credit-card-type business cards and club memberships. Explain that you represent some large club or company and are looking to move from paper to plastic cards. Ask for some samples. Expect about half a dozen samples, which usually will be examples of previous orders. The cards you receive obviously will not be high-level identification documents, but they could still prove extremely useful at some future date.

Look for the addresses of suitable printers/suppliers in the classified pages of business service magazines or the Yellow Pages. Note that with all such schemes, you needn't pay much attention if the ad requests a nominal payment for samples. Most companies will simply send the samples anyway, as this is less time consuming than writing back, asking for payment, and then sending the samples out. This simple request technique (especially if supported by impressive-looking letterhead) can also be used to get free catalogs from high-power companies that sell theirs at anywhere up to fifty dollars.

A useful selection of business cards can be obtained from their legitimate owners simply by asking at most any shop, show, exhibition, trade fair, and the like.

▼
FREE GASOLINE

A couple of techniques are described here. The first sees you back in the rental car. This time you are due to return it with a full tank of gas, as per many rental agreements. Instead of filling the tank up, however, locate the gas gauge sender (located on the top of the gas tank and accessible from the trunk). Lift up any carpeting and insulation material and check for a small connector with a wire leading from it. Remove this connector and the fuel gauge will read zero. Connect it to earth (by wedging it between the carpet/insulation and the sender securing screws, for example) and the gauge will read maximum.

An alternative is to undo the screws holding the sender unit in place and lift it out. Bend the float arm downward a couple of inches, thereby lowering its position. Now reaffix the sender on the tank. The gauge will now read much higher than it should and the vehicle can be returned with it showing full when, in reality, there is only a fraction of that amount in there. The extra effort required to accomplish this modification would be better rewarded if the vehicle were a large van or even a truck.

A perfectly legal way of getting free gas in this situation is to take advantage of the inherent inaccuracy of most gas gauges. You may well have noticed on your own vehicle that the gauge reads full for any number of actual levels above a certain minimum. Thus, instead of simply pumping gas until the pump shuts off because the gas is up to the base of the filler tube, have someone keep an eye on the gauge and stop as soon as it shows full. This will save you around a gallon or so on the majority of vehicles.

Another technique suitable for use when you can find a garage that doesn't padlock the pump nozzles after hours is to simply move from pump to pump and empty the gas that remains in each hose. You won't get much from each pump, but it is free and could mean the difference between being stranded and getting home.

Another technique requires the assistance of a helper and is applicable for situations in which you can access the emergency power cut-off box at a self-service petrol station. These are usually painted red and located on one side of the service station wall.

Arrange some covert signal with the helper and, just before your tank is full, give the signal, at which point he pulls the circuit breaker. This will instantly cut power to the pumps. The power is then restored and the helper departs. In the ensuing confusion, the staff will have little choice but to ask you how much gas you put in. You say something like, "Oh, I'm not sure but I was only topping up so it couldn't have been more than a couple of dollars or so."

It has also been discovered that certain levels and frequencies of RF (radio frequency) energy can interfere with many types of digital electronic equipment, including some gas pumps. The classified pages of several electronic hobbyist magazines have carried ads for modules of this type designed specifically to interfere with the CPUs (Central Processor Units) of digital circuits found in everything from gaming machines to gas pumps. In operation, these devices interfere with the control signals within the electronic system and cause it to shut down, restart from zero, or generally screw up. In any event, the RF-producing device is held close to the unit in question and triggered a couple of times to provoke a reaction. Rumor has it that a hand-held amateur radio transmitter operating at the upper-HF/lower-VHF frequencies will work as well.

Some people have even been known to steal gas from closed service stations by adapting a van so that a section of the floor can be lifted out and a long (ten to twenty-five foot) length of hose lowered through it. They park over the fuel storage tank filler, lift off the cover plate, unscrew the large sealing cap, then lower the hose into the underground tank and syphon fuel out with the use of a manual pump. Any passersby will only see a parked van and (especially if the hood is up and someone is apparently trying to fix a broken-down engine) take no notice at all.

▼

FREE GOURMET
LUNCHES

All you need to do is locate a convenient food or culinary college and drop them a line or phone about the chances of getting on the invitation list. Many such colleges have regular lunches to which members of the public are invited. This is done with a view to giving students real-life experience in preparing food for and serving food to customers proper as opposed to classmates and relatives.

There may be a waiting list and there may be a nominal fee. Consider any fee as a payment for the dessert and you get the main course for free. It may also be a case of knowing the right people, but it is certainly worth a letter or two or a personal visit.

FREE HAIR CARE

Free haircuts are available from various salons that train new hairstylists. Following the basic training, such persons are "set loose" on the public on a supervised basis. Since many people will shy away from having their hair done by a novice, the salons frequently offer free or, at the least, heavily discounted styling sessions.

For specific details, scan the local newspapers for ads or visit a few salons and ask. Always dress smartly and be polite.

At any salon you could always refuse to pay because you are unhappy with the results, or feign an inability to pay because you brought the wrong wallet/purse with you. What are they going to do, hold you till the hair grows back?!

FREE LIFT

A free lift from the majority of medium- and large-size hotels to the airport and vice versa can be obtained care of the various courtesy bus services that typically operate on an hourly basis. Look for signs at hotels and wait in the lobby (no one will ask any questions) or at the airport.

If you're a hitchhiker, free lifts can be obtained readily if you don a temporary arm sling and make a big show of struggling with your briefcase or whatever, or if you invest in a stick, bandage a leg, and limp pathetically. Explain to those that stop that your friend was giving you a lift but the car broke down and you simply must get to wherever by whenever.

▼

FREE MAGAZINES

Magazines are readily available by mail from the majority of publishers. All you need to do is write and explain that you are interested in taking out some quarter-page ads for your company, which sells any contextually appropriate item, and you would like to see what the editorials are like for the next couple of months. Request the advertising rate card as well. Using decent letterhead that "proves" you are the company you say you are is a must.

If you can find a nearby paper pulping mill, you can also get recent magazines and paperback books for free or, at the most, the cost of a drink. Literally hundreds of thousands of these are pulped each month, and most large pulping mills (or most other trade waste processing plants) will have tons of the things scattered about ready for disposal. Don't try and scrounge a van load of books or magazines, though; just enough for your own use.

▼
FREE MAILING
ADDRESSES

A temporary free mailing address can be obtained simply and legally by using the "poste restante" service offered by most post offices in most parts of the world. It sometimes pays to inquire at the office in question beforehand, but most times simply turning up at the office in question at about the time you expect the letter to arrive and asking if there is any poste restante mail for whomever will suffice. Be prepared to have to show some identification. If you do intend to visit the office beforehand, explain that you are just passing through and have no fixed address. Maybe you are camping.

Private companies that provide a mailing address service frequently offer a free trial period of several weeks or a month or so. Keep an eye on the classified ads in magazines and free papers. When contacting the company, inquire about annual fees and any other available services to give the impression that you are a potentially valuable customer.

▼

FREE MAPS AND GUIDES

These are available by mail from the tourist bureaus of the city, town, or country in question. Again, specific addresses can be found in the obvious directories, and a simple letter or phone call asking the cost of available items will work wonders. Mention that you are organizing a tour for a number of people and expect an even more varied selection of material.

Travel agencies will also be pleased to let you have any number of guides and maps if you imply that you intend to book the trip through them.

▼
FREE MEDICAL CARE

Certain types of free medical treatment are available in the majority of large cities at clinics operated in conjunction with university medical schools. There also exist many charitable clinics operating, sometimes on a sporadic basis, for the benefit of homeless persons and runaways, as well as special clinics that provide shots for specific communicable diseases. Addresses and details for these establishments are available from city health departments and community information centers.

Free treatment can also be had by visiting the on-campus clinics attached to large universities. Familiarize yourself with enough of the university setup to be able to answer basic questions concerning courses, professors, etc., and use fake I.D. as required.

If asked for I.D. that you don't have, explain that you don't have it with you and were just passing by and thought you'd pop in, as your whatever has been bothering you. Wince and sigh and offer to come back later with the I.D. Any medical staff member worth his/her salt will insist on checking you out there and then. Should the university carry medical records or computerized details of all students, explain that you have just transferred in and so probably won't be on the computer yet.

A similar technique can be used to obtain an examination, a prescription, or at least a flu shot from the clinics attached to large manufacturing and industrial plants. Simply pop in (wearing overalls or whatever, as appropriate) and describe the symptoms.

Medical treatment from doctors and hospital outpatient departments has been obtained for free on the strength of fake I.D. or simply by bypassing the cashier on the way out. If the cashier cannot be avoided, an excuse relating to how you were jogging and therefore not carrying funds or I.D. when the discomfort/pain started should be offered. Give a phony address with a request that the bill be sent there. Explanations pertaining to how you are from out of state and staying with friends, or how he has just returned from several months overseas, etc., would be offered to fend off questions about why the usual family doctor was not used.

FREE MONEY

Ah! So you thought you'd skip everything else and read this section first, eh? Okay, fair enough. But you do realize that you've missed the "free gift" telephone number on page seven, don't you?

Back again, huh? Okay, so there isn't any free gift number. That'll teach you to be greedy.

I did promise, however, so here are details of where you can go to get free money—money that people have thrown away. Yes, really. The "secret" location in question is . . . almost any public fountain. Yep, we've all seen them, throwing and wishing, throwing and wishing.

I can see the romantic attraction of some two-hundred-year-old Venetian fountain, but what possible gods of luck can be invoked via the steel and concrete efforts dotting most every shopping mall or airport? If you stop and ask these people if they are deliberately contributing to the local authority or fountain cleaner's fund, my guess is that most of them will say no. It's just that some sort of tradition has developed whereby people see a fountain and throw money into it.

So, the free money may be collected at any convenient time by simply reaching in and taking it. You might even want to deposit a thin, white net, weighted at the corners with lead shot, in a popular fountain and retrieve it when it's sufficiently covered. If the fountain sports some sign which specifically states that money therein will be donated to a charity, then leave it alone. There are plenty of others that attract money by default.

Another method of obtaining free money is to construct a collecting box or can of the type used by charity workers. Label the box/can with the name of your chosen good cause and fix it, using any expedient method, close to a newspaper vending machine. Keep a covert eye on the box and recover it after a few hours. Expect a lot of people who have dug out change for the paper to put a few coins in the box. Give half of what you make to a real charity.

Never, as some people do, take the box to large public events and solicit for donations by rattling the can like a genuine collector. Having said that, if you clearly mark the can with something like, "Don't put money in here, please," I can't see how anyone can accuse you of doing anything dishonest. Rest assured that at big, crowded events, even if you mark the can, "Buzz off you moron," you will still get people stuffing coins into it.

Free money might also be obtained by investing in an ad in a popular magazine that offers extremely cheap advertising in another paper. Offer the ads at a cost far below the usual price and be sure to specify the applicable word limit, etc. When the ads and payment are received, resubmit them to any of the numerous free papers that you can find that also offer free ad service, which is most of them. If you think about it, this is a legitimate service, as the advertiser may well be getting exposure in a paper he would not normally have access to. It is only fair to charge a small fee for this service.

Two hundred and fifty dollars has been collected for free by several people who have "lost" an item of luggage when traveling by air. The technique used was to travel with a friend and check at least one item of baggage in at the desk. Then, upon their arrival at the destination, have the friend walk off with it as if it were his or her own. Rarely does anyone check; luggage is simply pulled from the conveyor belt by its owner and carted off.

Ultimately a check will be made, of course, to see if a claimant did check a bag in, and a record of its weight will be available.

This should be borne in mind by persons making claims for luggage "lost" in this manner; if the check-in receipt showed the case weighed only twenty pounds and the items claimed to be in it totaled a lot more, suspicions might be aroused.

As it is certain that a surveillance camera is monitoring the luggage claim area, the poor, distressed traveler should make a show of looking for his bag and then asking everyone he can find where it might be. Eventually he or she reports it as missing at the appropriate desk (along with much shouting and promises never to use that airline again), the baggage check-in receipt is handed over, some forms are filled out, and a month or so later a check for the claimed value turns up in the mail. The airline will simply assume that the case was misrouted, stolen by handlers, or lifted either deliberately or accidentally by another traveler.

The people using the technique should take care to act as strangers when departing the aircraft and waiting at the baggage claim carousel. The case should contain only clothing, books, magazines, etc., and no identifying documents or papers. There should be no name tag attached. On international flights, the "nothing to declare" line should be selected. Even if the carrier is stopped and the case searched, nothing unusual would be discovered.

People have also used a home or office break-in to make free money by exaggerating the value of items stolen to the insurance company or claiming that certain items that weren't stolen were. Claims for things that didn't even exist have been made as well and, providing the amount claimed is not excessive and the correct type of policy had been selected, no one is ever any the wiser. Sometimes a company will ask for receipts for items claimed on a nonspecified type of policy. Unless the contractual small print indicates that this is a requirement, tell them to get lost. Who the hell keeps receipts for everything anyway, and who would have a receipt if the item was a gift or purchased from a stall at a fair?

Assuming the break-in is reported to the police, and assuming that no ridiculous claims as to the value of items stolen are made, there will rarely be a problem.

Unscrupulous people have also been known to "lose" traveler's checks and credit cards to friends or cohorts, who then use them before serial numbers and other details can be circulated. The checks and cards should be used shortly after they are reported lost or stolen to the police, and about the same time as or shortly before they are reported lost to the issuing authority.

The return from the checks or goods purchased on the credit card is divided between "loser" and user. The intelligent perpetrator of this type of scam will limit the "loss" to hundreds rather than thousands of dollars and will not repeat the exercise.

People engaged in the selling of scrap metal, car bodies, etc., have been known to "load" the material in question with sand, stones, lead, or even concrete. This technique is particularly applicable to situations in which the buyer employs a simple weigh-in scheme where the vehicle carrying the scrap is driven onto a bridge and weighed, the scrap unloaded, the vehicle alone weighed again, and the difference (which is the weight of the scrap) used as the basis for payment. This process frequently is accompanied by only a cursory inspection of the material with a view to determining its nature and base value.

In this situation the various cavities in vehicle bodies (the fuel tank and pipework, for example) are used to conceal the "loading." The trick, as it were, is to add only enough material to earn a few free dollars rather than trying to double the weight of the material. This is relative, however, and the larger the quantity of scrap, the larger the potential free earnings.

▼

FREE MORNING PAPER WITH COFFEE AND DONUTS

Free morning newspapers, coffee, and donuts are available in the majority of medium-price-range hotels and motels. Many offer this service in the morning only, some all day long. Arrive in the morning around 8:45 and enter the lobby via the car park or through any door that is obviously more likely to be used by guests than new arrivals. Smile and say hi to anyone on duty at the desk that catches your eye. Be confident. Help yourself to coffee and a donut and settle yourself down for a pleasant read of the morning news. Don't walk off with the newspaper. I might want it.

▼

FREE MOVIE POSTERS AND PHOTOS

You can get a nice selection of these by writing to the publicity departments of studios and film production companies. Addresses can be found in the usual directories and on the cases or labels of video cassettes. Explain that you would welcome any material relating to new productions for use as prizes for a competition you will soon be running in some film club magazine.

Posters are also to be had from video rental stores, who get inundated with the things each month. Material relating to the previous month's releases is usually thrown in the garbage. Ask at the shops themselves or write to distribution companies directly and ask what they have available.

▼

FREE PARCEL
DELIVERY

Free long-distance parcel delivery by rail or bus is obtained by similar means. The first requirement is that the parcel is contained within an easily carried piece of luggage such as a suitcase. Further, the delivery is prearranged and the recipient briefed as to where and at what time the package is to arrive and what name the case identity tag carries.

In the case of delivery by rail, the technique involves accessing the appropriate train courtesy of a platform ticket and depositing the package in an overhead locker not already being used (or, more specifically, not filled to capacity) by another passenger. There should, however, be a passenger traveling to the same destination as the package seated beneath or close to the locker you select.

This is easily achieved simply by watching until a passenger or three have settled themselves and then entering the train. With your best smile, inquire of a passenger as to his or her destination. Assuming this is the required destination, place the suitcase in the locker and ask if they would mind keeping an eye on it, as you intend to travel with your friend/elderly mother/whomever seated further down the train, but the luggage racks are full down there.

Thank them profusely and leave, exiting the train out of sight of them. Now call the person to whom the parcel is being sent and give them the car and seat number and the estimated arrival time of the train. They will meet the train, access it as if meeting some-one, and retrieve the case, having ready a few kind words of thanks for the passenger who has been keeping an eye on it. They will be too concerned with collecting their own items together and leaving the train to analyze why the person collecting the case is not the person who deposited it (assuming they notice in the first place).

For delivery by bus, it is necessary only to turn up at the depot or pick-up point and offer the bag for stowage along with those of the legitimate passengers. Typically, no ticket will be asked for until one actually tries to board the bus or until it is under way, depending on the service. The driver or the ticket collector stow-ing the bags will ask for the destination since they are stowed on a last-out/first-in basis. Once the case is on, hover around and then depart as if you have been seeing someone off.

Again, it will be unusual for anyone to ask awkward ques-tions. The guy stowing the bags will assume that if you are not the traveler then you are loading the bag for someone who is. This impression can be reinforced by smiling and waving through the bus window as if to an already-seated friend. Once again, call the person who is to collect the parcel and give them time details, etc.

A variation on this technique is to wait until a bus for the required destination pulls out and, when certain that there is no chance of you actually stopping it, run out after it shouting and brandishing the case. Attract lots of attention and then find the station manager/ticket inspector.

Explain that Mr. X, who is from out of state and has been stay-ing with you for a few days, has left his case. You didn't realize until the last minute and rushed out to try and get it to him. What'll you do? He'll be in a terrible mess without it. Just a minute, would it be possible to put the case on the next coach out? You could then call the guy when he gets home and tell him the case can be collected from the coach depot down there. It would? Great! Thanks very much!

▼

FREE PETS

Pet cats and dogs are available free from the various animal shelters. The only requirement usually is that you can provide a good home. Such shelters are not keen on giving you a large dog, however, if you live on the thirty-eighth floor of an apartment building and work all day.

Many private individuals also give away pets of various types that have become too expensive to keep, or when the novelty of having the pet has worn off. Thus, a free "Wanted" ad in the local free paper for whatever will often turn up offers of everything from fish and spiders to parakeets.

▼
FREE PHONE CALLS

Extremely short free phone calls can be obtained perfectly legally via the operator. Although short, they can still, for example, be useful for letting a contact overseas know that you are home after a trip away, or that you agree to some previously discussed offer, and so on.

All you need to do is work out a simple code beforehand and when you make the call (which will be made collect via the operator), use it to pass the message. For example, call the operator and ask for a reverse-charge call to "Mr. Stephen Higgins." The operator calls the number and asks for the person in question. Your contact answers that Mr. Higgins is not available. The operator relays this to you and you thank her/him and hang up.

"Mr. Higgins," of course, does not exist but is a prearranged code meaning whatever you like. The message has been passed over what might be thousands of miles and it hasn't cost you a penny.

Another possibility is for you to ask to make a reverse-charge call to "Mr. Green." The operator calls the number and says, "I have a collect call for Mr. Green from Mr. Whomever. Will you accept the charges?" Your contact pauses and then says something like, "Oh, sorry, this is Mr. Green's office but he's not actually here/is in the hospital/will not be back until tomorrow/whatever. I can't accept the call, I'm afraid." The operator passes this back to you and the call is concluded. The required message has, however, already been passed!

A variation that might still work in some areas is to have the person you want to speak to standing by in a phone booth at an agreed time. You know the number of this booth. You call the operator and ask to make a collect call to the number of the booth. When the operator calls, the person answers and agrees to accept the charges as if it were a private phone.

In some areas this technique is unworkable because the phone system is so sophisticated it will alert the operator to the fact that the number is that of a pay phone, and in other areas the ringer on the phone has been disconnected. If this latter technique is suspected, it can be circumvented by good timing. Often a pay phone will have a special suffix that identifies it as a pay phone. If this is in addition to the usual area code and number sequence, then simply don't give it when you ask to make the reverse-charge call. If you are asked if the number you are calling is a pay phone, answer that you really couldn't say, you were given the number by a friend as a contact for a job, or suchlike.

If the phone booths in your part of the world have no numbers shown on the dial, they can be determined by having someone make a collect call to you from one. When answering the operator, explain that you are just cleaning up and will be available in a few minutes. You don't want to accept the charge but can you have the number please so you can return the call shortly? In any event, each booth will have a finite useable life, as at some point the phone company will realize that it is sending bills to itself.

Another method is to obtain a phone credit card and, using it as a reference, construct a variant with another number so that the charges get billed to someone else or, in the event you hit on a number sequence that hasn't been issued, nobody. Never use this method from your home or business phone, only from a pay phone.

It is even possible to establish your very own free telephone network for use by friends in the same or a nearby neighborhood. The "phones" used are those FM intercom units of the type available from Radio Shack and elsewhere. Although intended for interoffice or room-to-room communication, most such units are capable of transmitting for distances of a quarter mile or so. This is providing, however, that the electric sockets into which they are plugged at the different locations share the same mains phasing. For greater distances, two units can be used as a sort of "repeater"—one receives a signal at the limit of its range and retransmits it at a restored power on down the line.

▼
FREE PIZZAS

If you get really desperate for a pizza, one can be had for free from any of the outlets that offer a "delivery within thirty minutes or you don't pay" deal. You will need a helper with a vehicle, and you should ideally be located at the limit of the delivery area.

Your helper watches until the delivery vehicle approaches and then cuts it off, "stalls" in front of it, or flags it down by flashing the headlights, sounding the horn, and pointing. When the delivery van pulls over, the helper will explain that he thought he saw flames coming from beneath the vehicle. He must have been mistaken, sorry. The delivery van will be held up for just long enough to make the thirty-minute deadline impossible. When the pizza is delivered, insist that the company stick to its advertised policy and don't pay. If you feel really guilty, offer to pay half. That way you get half a pizza for free and your conscience won't hurt you half as much.

FREE PLANTS

Countless varieties of garden plants can be obtained for free from any number of public or private parks. The displayed plants are frequently changed from season to season, and those that are dug out invariably end up on the compost heap. Simply cultivate the friendship of one of the gardeners working in such places and ask politely.

Another source is from the gardens of people who are leaving the area. Keep an eye open for people moving out and leaving the garden plants behind. Ask if you might have some of them, commenting that it seems a shame to have them die from neglect when they could be going to a good home.

▼

FREE POSTAGE

Free postage can be secured by having a few friends who write to you frequently do so, but with the letters addressed to a name other than your own. The return name and address should be that of the persons to whom you intend to write for free. Have the senders leave the envelopes tucked in rather than stuck down.

When they arrive, replace the letters with your own, write "gone away" across your address, and drop them in the mailbox. The letters will be returned to the "sender," who are, of course, the people you actually want to receive the letters anyway.

An alternative is to use the postpaid official or company envelopes that are supplied with statements, bills, demands, or offers from government departments or large distributors of products. Simply affix a typed address label over any existing address or, if applicable, fold your letter to fit and write the address on the back so that it is visible through the window and mail. Using government envelopes for private mail is a crime if you work for the government. It is probably illegal if you don't, too.

With certain stamps that have already passed through the system, it is possible to remove the ink and reuse the stamp. This is especially applicable when the canceling machine has only caught a section of the stamp, as is often the case, or where the cancellation mark is simply a date/time mark rather than a message or some description.

Any number of methods can be used to remove the ink. These range from simple, careful washing with warm water and detergent to the use of ink removal liquids, lemon juice, acetic acid, etc. The final stage of all such projects is to rinse the stamp under clean water, blot between two sheets of absorbent white paper, and then allow to air dry.

A quick spray of artist's adhesive or some similar glue will reaffix the stamp to an envelope. The stamp ink is surprisingly resilient and will take much more abuse than might be imagined. Be aware, however, that the stamps of some countries may incorporate some type of concealed security mark which makes it possible for either sophisticated electronic scanning systems and/or manual inspection personnel to confirm that a given stamp has or has not been previously used.

By arranging for friends who send you letters to put the stamps in the wrong corner of the envelope (bottom left is best, as this is an easily made mistake if the stamp was affixed before the envelope was addressed), you will end up with a supply of uncanceled stamps that can be removed by soaking or with the old steam kettle method. They can then be reused if attached with a light adhesive (although if steam is used to remove the stamp, in many cases enough original adhesive remains to enable it to be placed onto another envelope).

▼

FREE PRODUCE

Tons of perfectly good produce is thrown away each day at wholesale markets since, if the perishable food isn't sold, it is unlikely to be fit for the next day. Sometimes the span is a few days, but in any event at some point all sorts of good stuff is tossed. Wholesale market produce is rarely, if ever, sold at a discount because if it were, no one would buy it at the full price—they would just wait for the "sell by" date to draw near again.

It is unlikely that many of you will ever need to scrounge basic produce from the wholesale markets simply to survive. If you do, I can sympathize, as I have done it myself in the past. More likely, however, is that you want to obtain a few examples of some of the more expensive, exotic fruits and vegetables. These are available, and if your timing is right you will end up with a huge box of the stuff simply for the asking, as you will be saving a worker the trouble of collecting it up and taking it to the rubbish bin.

▼
FREE RADIO
PROGRAMS

Several international broadcast stations and various organizations (including the United Nations, who might even send you a video or two if you ask nicely) offer free programs for use by other stations operating outside of their primary target audience area. The subject matter will vary and conditions of use are imposed. For example, some of the available material will carry a requirement that it is broadcast only once and before a certain date, and most suppliers point out that the programs must not be used in conjunction with advertising.

Radio Netherlands, Radio Moscow, and *Deutsche Welle* (The Voice of Germany), among others, offer this service. Specific station addresses can be obtained from the *World Radio and Television Handbook*, available from most large booksellers and specialist shops catering to the shortwave listener/amateur radio community.

You will need to write on letterhead that identifies you as a public service station, a charitable organization, or some similar group having a legitimate requirement. In any case, full details and a multilingual catalog of available material will be sent.

When writing to organizations, explain that you have an interest in their work, purpose, and achievements, and request details of any available audio/visual information packages. Saying that you represent a general discussion group that is always on the

---

lookout for new topics and sources of information will work wonders. Always enclose something for the return postage or some International Reply Coupons when you write.

FREE RECORDS

Free records can be obtained from many large record companies (and even more from the smaller, independent ones) simply by writing and requesting that you be placed on the promotional distribution list.

Use a letterhead that shows you to be the editor of a new music magazine or the director of a new radio station and explain that the magazine/station is to have a particular bias toward the type of music produced by the company in question.

▼
FREE RESTAURANT MEALS

Free meals frequently can be obtained by adopting the guise of a reporter/reviewer for some food magazine or trade directory. Props include a briefcase, a notebook/cassette recorder, and a degree of acting ability. You should be very smartly dressed.

Enter the restaurant and be very obvious about looking around. Make notes or comments into the recorder, pausing only when approached by a waiter. Study the menu in detail and make more notes.

If you know anything about food, then ask the waiter detailed questions about how certain dishes are prepared. Make more notes. Ask the waiter how long he has worked there and how long the place has been under the present management. Make more notes.

Word will spread to the kitchen and the manager and about this time (if it has not already happened) you will be asked who you are and what you are doing. Answer that you are the food and drink reporter for some magazine or trade directory and that you have been charged to assess the standard of food and service in various establishments in the area for an upcoming article. Explain that the magazine/directory has a readership of several hundred thousand, etc.

Order the meal and make yet more notes. After the coffee you will be asked if you enjoyed the meal. Answer that you did and that it is a pleasant change to receive such good service. Expect now a visit from the manager, who will solicit your opinions and try to get an idea of the review you will be writing about his establishment. Explain that, although you shouldn't really tell him, the review will be more than favorable and you intend to give it the highest rating possible.

Tell him that you can, if he wishes, send a framed copy of the review for display. Expect him to agree and ask the cost. Explain that there will be no charges involved. If all has gone as planned, you will now be told that the meal is on the house. Thank him profusely and leave.

A variation is to determine the name of some magazine that the restaurant advertises in and have business cards made to identify you as a reviewer/feature writer for it. Ask at the onset if it will be possible to interview the manager/chef/waiter after the meal, as you have been asked to feature the restaurant in a soon-to-be-published article.

The other approach is to take a couple of guests with you to the restaurant. Small, white, furry guests to be precise. The mice should be concealed in a briefcase, air holes having been drilled into the base to ensure their comfort. At some point toward the end of the meal, release the mice and shout like hell. Stand up in a huff, throw down your knife and fork in disgust, and feign nausea.

Leave amidst the confusion and apologies from restaurant staff. In the unlikely event you are pressed for payment, roar adamantly that you do not usually pay for the privilege of dining with rodents! Mention the media, the health inspector, and the possibility of suing for psychological stress—what if the mouse had been on the food you ate! You'll be surprised how quickly they change their minds.

A free meal in the "All you can eat for five dollars" type of place can be had by using some deft footwork (or, more precisely, platework) if there are at least a couple of you working together. The technique is simply to seat yourselves at a table. When the waitress approaches, does a quick head count, and asks, "Three?" one of you replies, "Nope, just two. This guy's still pigged out from lunch/breakfast/whatever." The waitress smiles and gives you the bill for two people. The paying guys now cycle through the routine of getting food, and when there is a sufficient confusion of plates on the table (and whilst keeping an eye open for the real mean types who take the "No Sharing" signs too literally), the nonpayer can dig in.

In the larger, busier type of place that offers a fixed-price, all-you-can-eat service as well as standard pricing for other items, it is possible to order one meal, then sidle up to the counter twenty or thirty minutes later and select the fixed-price options. When you leave, simply present the cheaper of the bills at the cash register. Be sure to tip the cashier, as this practically guarantees that even if she has seen the scam go down she won't say anything.

▼

FREE SALT, PEPPER, AND OTHER CONDIMENTS

A variety of condiments are available free from any number of cafes, restaurants, and diners that provide such products in single-portion packets and pouches rather than conventional dispensers and bowls. Simply help yourself to the items displayed on the table and use on your next picnic or as emergency reserves at home. These packets are also of great use to hikers, campers, and such.

The adage, "Don't kick the backside out of it!" applies here, so don't start loading up bags and boxes with the stuff. You will be able to obtain without hassle more than you will ever really need, so don't get greedy.

▼

FREE SOAPS, SHAMPOOS, AND BUBBLE BATH

Masses of this stuff are available from the manufacturers that supply the hotel and motel industry. Check out the maker's name on a few such products (which are available free from the rest rooms of large hotels) or invest in a copy of a hotel or catering industry trade magazine and write a few letters. Invite samples with a view to your selecting a supplier for the chain of hotels/motels your company has just purchased.

FREE SUPERMARKET THINGS

Most supermarkets sport displays which are little more than accidents waiting to happen. The classic pyramid of cans is still to be found, as is a variety of box displays and special promotional signs. These are all designed to attract business. The last thing the market manager wants is an accident that generates bad publicity. So, should you stumble against a stack of cans, bang your head against some sign, or have some other accident (caused, of course, by the careless positioning of such a display), do not hesitate to call it to the manager's attention.

Express dismay that such and such would be set up at such a place and limp, rub a bruised arm, or nurse an aching head accordingly. Explain that although you were here to shop, you don't really feel up to it now. Maybe you'd better come back tomorrow, or maybe go somewhere else, it might be safer. Having a helper on hand to play the part of another shopper can work wonders. Have them mutter loudly about how they thought the display was stupid/dangerous too. If they were you, they'd sue. Explain that you don't see any need for that, and are more interested in getting the shopping done. Expect a bag of free groceries.

▼

FREE TELEVISED SHOWS

You can get free tickets for many popular television shows by writing to the production company studios and asking. It's as simple as that, but expect to wait anywhere up to a few months and remember that several shows now on the air were actually recorded in front of a live audience some time ago. Mark the letter to the attention of the Ticketing Division. An alternative is to ask the operator to check if the company has a separate number for ticket inquiries. You can then call them directly and see what tickets are currently available.

▼
FREE "THINGS THAT HAVE THOSE BAR CODE PRICE LABELS" ON THEM

The bar code is that small, black-and-white stripey thing you see stuck on everything nowadays, from food to rental cars. It carries information pertaining to the product itself and the price, etc. It is read by a bar-code reader, which might be the hand-held type or a fixed type, as in the case of store checkouts where the merchandise is passed over the reader beam.

Ever noticed the speed with which such products are passed over that beam? Fast, huh? It has to be or the investment in technology would be wasted. The item is passed over the beam, the price is added to the total (and the store inventory computer data base is updated), and the item is placed into a bag.

Now, if someone was to arm himself with a few custom-made stickers of the right size and shape and affix them, surreptitiously, over existing stickers or labels, what do you think would happen? Right! As long as they didn't go mad and try to alter a five dollar item to fifty cents, they should have no problem and no one would even notice that the jar contains real caviar and not the cheaper imitation. Someone need only do this to a few things and they've got half their purchases for free.

The easiest technique is to note the value of bar codes by comparing them to the actual cost of the items and then remove the labels, cut out the codes, and photocopy a few. You might even have some professionally printed. The printer will simply think the order was from a legitimate dealer (if he bothers to think anything at all). Photocopied codes could be sprayed on back with artist's adhesive and a piece of waxed paper placed over this until the sticker is needed.

▼

FREE TRAIN TRAVEL

This technique could be used to get free passage after having accessed the train with a platform ticket or to get a better class of travel such as first class with only a second-class ticket.

The accessories used here are a priest's collar, a suitable black collarless shirt, and a nicely embossed and very obvious Bible. Glasses and a hat seem to help also. Quite simply, all you do is position yourself for the journey in your selected car and some time before the ticket collector comes around, pretend to fall asleep. If the car is empty then you can slip into this deep sleep at the last minute. If the car is occupied, then drop off a bit more naturally.

Have the Bible in a conspicuous position on your lap and, if all goes well, the ticket collector, after a couple of gentle attempts at waking you, will leave you in peace. If you are awakened, however, and the collector is insistent that you produce a valid ticket, keep up the bluff and the worst that should happen is that your fake I.D. details will be noted, albeit with some regret on the part of the collector, for subsequent action.

The uniform of a railway worker also can be used to good effect on certain lines. Come prepared with a bag of tools and some ready chat. Keep out of the way of the ticket collector if at all possible but, if cornered and pressed for an explanation as to your identity, simply explain that there have been complaints about the security of the door locks/windows/noise levels/whatever from "engineering" and you are the manufacturer's maintenance man.

Waffle on about being overworked and underpaid and you should have no hassles. The secret of success in all similar situations is to be talkative and friendly and to press the other guy for conversation. Dropping things into the conversation like, "I mean, you're the expert, surely. You're the guy who knows the score. If you haven't reported anything I can't see what the problem is."

The typical reaction to this will be either agreement or comments to the effect that he is too busy with his own job to notice stuff like that. If this happens, jump back in with something like, "Exactly. You guys deserve twice the wage. Christ, it's getting harder to make ends meet, huh?"

Researching the name of the manufacturer of the cars a few days prior to the day of travel will work wonders. You can have some sort of impressive I.D. card made up for use as an emergency trump card. Make sure the date of issue is some time in the future, however, and mistreat the card so as to create the impression of age and wear and tear.

Since you won't want to be stuck wearing work clothes when you reach your destination, a change of clothes and any other personal belongings can be placed in a briefcase and deposited in a luggage rack upon boarding.

For many people who are traveling with a friend or a group of friends, free train travel can be achieved as follows. At least one ticket is purchased. The person who is to travel free (or at half price, usually, if traveling with a friend) gets on the train with a platform ticket. When the train leaves, "float" until you have determined from which direction the ticket collector is starting his round. At this stage the ticket holder seats himself so as to ensure that he will be asked for a ticket long before the other person, who positions himself at an agreed location much further down the train.

When the available ticket is requested, the holder makes sure that he will be remembered by the collector by engaging him in conversation, cracking some joke, or pretending that he is having trouble locating the ticket. In any event, it will be produced and clipped. A minute or so later the holder leaves his position and moves down the train to the person traveling for free.

The ticket is handed over and the new holder now walks back down the train past the collector to a seat location in an area already cleared by the collector. If this person should be stopped and asked for a ticket, it would be produced confidently with a comment along the lines of, "Not again. You just clipped it back there!" (indicating in the direction from which the collector has come).

It is extremely unlikely that the collector will be certain enough that he hasn't clipped that person's ticket to make a fuss. To eliminate the risk of any small suspicion being amplified, however, the two parties involved in the project should not sit together during the journey.

The rail authorities in many countries now offer travel pass deals to foreign visitors which save them so much off usual prices that most of the journeys obtained in this manner can honestly be called free. The passes are only available outside of the country in which they are to be used, but if you have a friend abroad you might want to ask him to check out the offers at the local travel agents. Similar passes are available for air travel.

▼

FREE TURNSTILE ACCESS

Simplicity itself, this, yet some people still insist on jumping, crawling, or climbing over, under, or around turnstiles and thereby attracting lots of attention to themselves. There again, under cover of others or if concealed by pillars, etc., the athletic approach might still prove useful. A far better way, however, to pass through most any turnstile that opens when a coin or ticket is inserted is just to squash up close to the person in front of you. If with a friend, take turns paying so the other gets in free. If operating alone, wait until the turnstile is just opening and then "accidentally" push the guy in front so that you clear the bars as well. Always apologize profusely and say that you tripped or were yourself pushed.

In situations where jumping or climbing quickly over a turnstile is an option but for the beady eye of a nearby security guard or other watcher, distraction techniques are often used with great effect. The persons (usually two or three) who are to jump the turnstile take up positions as if they are about to insert a coin or ticket, as applicable. A helper positioned on the opposite side of the watcher suddenly screams some name at the top of his voice (as if he had spotted someone in the distance). As the watcher turns to look, the others jump over.

▼

FREE TYPEWRITER AND PRINTER RIBBONS

Used typewriter ribbons are regularly discarded by companies, and a brief visit to the bin/Dumpster area will turn up dozens of them. Although not really worth the effort to professional users, fabric typewriter and printer ribbons can be given a new lease on life when re-inked with commercially available sprays. Tins of inking spray can be purchased for about eight dollars and contain enough material to ink a typical ribbon up to twenty times. The cost of the spray, therefore, is easily recouped.

At least one free ribbon can usually be had without investing in inking spray by spraying the "dead" ribbon with some of the WD-40 you have lying around in the garage.

FREE VEHICLE INSURANCE

Several noncomprehensive vehicle insurance policies incorporate a clause that permits the insured to drive any other vehicle that is not owned by or hired to him under a rental agreement. This type of policy can be exploited legally in parts of the world where there is a legal distinction between a vehicle's owner and its registered keeper.

Where applicable, this "loophole" allows, for example, your spouse to purchase a V8 Rocket (thereby becoming the legal owner) and loan it to you on a long-term basis, as long as you complete the proper papers and thereby become the registered keeper. If you already have insurance on your straight-four clunker and the policy sports the type of clause described above, you can legally drive the V8 for a fraction of the insurance premium it would otherwise cost.

The downside of this technique is that the vehicle technically would not be covered against fire or theft, only third-party accidents.

▼
FREE VIDEOTAPES

New film and music releases can be obtained by having some letterhead printed up that shows you to be the producer of a new cable or satellite television film review program or the movie/music reviewer for some new video magazine or club. As with all such products, producers and distributors are only too eager to secure additional publicity, and free promotional material is accounted for in all but the poorest of advertising budgets.

Less scrupulous individuals have been known to secure free videotapes by copying rental films. Many video production companies incorporate some form of copy protection system so that if you try to copy VCR to VCR in the usual fashion, nothing but garbage appears on the duplicate tape. "Black boxes" are available, however, that defeat many of these protection systems, but a cheaper alternative used by some people is to copy via the RF socket. This means they are copying a modulated radio frequency signal (as would normally appear at the antenna socket of the television or VCR) rather than the scrambled audio and video signals.

FREE WAGES

This is an old technique, but it is still used by employees of certain large companies. The success of the technique relies on the fact that few large companies perceive a need to check on an individual basis which employees have been working overtime and which have not and, in many cases, whether an employee has actually been present for the full working day at all. Clock-in cards simply are processed by the wages department and, unless some particularly unusual combination of hours worked or missed occurs, no verification is made. Thus if a job can be completed in half a day rather than the allotted full day, it is possible for a worker to leave at lunchtime and have a friend punch him back in for the afternoon.

Similarly, a co-worker can "forget" to punch out at the end of the normal working day and have a friend who is working overtime anyway clock both cards when he leaves. Traditionally, the persons involved in such an arrangement take turns covering each other.

Contract managers, supervisors, and others responsible for submitting hours-worked details on behalf of department members have frequently arranged with one or more employees to exaggerate the number of hours worked in return for the lion's share of the subsequent payment. Similarly, completely fictitious returns have been made on behalf of nonexistent employees, although the period of "employment" is kept short so that by the time the paperwork comes to be processed the "employee" has "left" again! This latter technique works well with subcontract companies employing a high proportion of casual or part-time workers and in companies where the pay is poor and staff turnover high. Contract office cleaning and industrial cleaning companies are examples.

A variation on the theme occurs when a department member leaves. The rest of the team agrees to share the wages (or the supervisor/manager keeps it all himself) and the work is covered by the remaining personnel. In a similar vein, certain contractors will sign a contract with employers based on a given number of workers and never produce anywhere near that number to do the work. The extra pay may sometimes be used to "sweeten" the actual employees' pay, though often it simply goes straight into the contractor's pocket.

FREE X RAYS

Chest X rays can be obtained from various free preventative medicine clinics that are maintained by most cities. The best bet is to check out a current phone directory for listings under Public Health and Health Education, or call a local district health center and ask for information about free clinics.

Having determined what, if any, conditions must be met to qualify for a free examination (the common denominator here will usually be a lack of funds or insurance coverage so, if appropriate, dress down and prepare a reasonable background story), pay a visit to the place and describe your chest pains. Some free private clinics operate in many cities as well, as do certain university clinics.

FREE YACHT TRIPS

Free yacht voyages often can be obtained by scanning the advertising pages of nautical magazines for "Crew Wanted" ads. Even completely inexperienced personnel sometimes are recruited for certain trips, although there will be no pay and there invariably is a fitness requirement. If you have some basic sailing experience, so much the better. Placing a want ad for employment of this type might also work, but forget any ideas of a lazy sail in the sun. You will have to work very hard indeed.

A technique calling for slightly less energy expenditure is to look for ads or place your own for yacht security personnel. Piracy is still rife on many of the world's seas and armed security personnel in such places are an essential requirement.

▼

FREE ZOO VISITS

Most zoos charge an admission fee, but there usually are a couple of free ones in or close to big cities. Check out tourist information material and you might be pleasantly surprised at the amount of free entertainment available right in your backyard that you would not have heard about under normal circumstances.

In situations where there is a fee charged, apply the "Free Admission" techniques described earlier or contact a local orphanage or any child-related charity and offer to take a party of kids to the zoo on an expenses-paid basis. Explain that, although you would like to, you can't afford the expense yourself but, should it be of use, you would be pleased to offer your services.

A variation applicable not only to zoos but also to carnivals and the like is to make a written or verbal approach to the proprietors that explains how nice it would be if they could see their way to offering free admission for a party of deprived/disadvantaged kids. If you can tie this end down first, you can then approach a local children's charity and offer them the trip for free.

Many such charities own their own transportation but frequently are short of volunteer drivers and helpers. Establishing contact with such a group can be a great way to get all sorts of free things, from food at parties to theme park admission, while doing something positive for the community as well.